Man's Impossibility
God's
Possibility

Kenneth W. Hagin

Unless otherwise indicated, all Scripture quotations are taken from the *King James Version* of the Bible.

22 21 20 19 18 17 16   19 18 17 16 15 14 13

Man's Impossibility—God's Possibility
ISBN-13: 978-0-89276-700-7
ISBN-10: 0-89276-700-6

In the U.S. write:
Kenneth Hagin Ministries
P.O. Box 50126
Tulsa, OK 74150-0126
1-888-28-FAITH
rhema.org

In Canada write:
Kenneth Hagin Ministries of Canada
P.O. Box 335, Station D
Etobicoke (Toronto), Ontario
Canada M9A 4X3
1-866-70-RHEMA
rhemacanada.org

This book is respectfully and lovingly dedicated to my father, Kenneth E. Hagin. His influence on my life and ministry is a priceless blessing.

Contents

CHAPTER 1

Possibility Faith

Many times as we live our lives here on earth we hear these words over, and over, and over again: *impossible, impossible, impossible, impossible, impossible*. Listen to conversations all around you. You will hear it over and over again, but it doesn't have to be *impossible*. Even with the natural human, sense knowledge faith, sense realm, or head faith—whatever you want to call it, it doesn't have to be *impossible*.

Impossible? No. You can do something about it.

If **you believe**, you can **accomplish** something. It was said to the Wright Brothers, "You can't fly." But they did! According to what men said, there could not be a Golden Gate bridge in San Francisco. "Why, it's impossible!" It's there. The engineers were told, "You can't build Hoover Dam. It's impossible! It's too high! There is too much water to control. There is too much of a gorge." But they did! I have been there. I have stood on top of that dam and looked at it. I have driven across the Golden Gate bridge in a car. They told the engineers, "You're crazy! You shouldn't even attempt such a job."

The engineers said, "It is possible. It can be done. We believe it can be done." And they did it!

Several years ago when the scientists began to talk about going to the moon, and orbiting around the moon, newspaper articles (I read them) said, "Aw! I don't believe we will ever go to the moon. We can't go to the moon! Whoever heard of such an idiotic idea? Go to the moon? How in the world can we get out of the gravitational pull of the earth? We can't do that!"

But they did! Then they recanted and said, "Well, I guess they have made it that far." Then somebody wrote an article, saying, "Scientists are thinking about landing and walking on the moon! Don't they know they can't do that? Impossible!"

But they did! That is what natural human faith will get you. Many of you, who are reading these words, have gotten many things in life because you believed that you could do it. You were told that it was impossible but you did it anyway. You had a natural human faith, a faith that accomplished because you believed in yourself. It accomplished a goal for you. You set out to do a job, and you did the job because you believed in yourself.

Some things are impossible for man to do.

Now, I want you to notice that regardless of how much natural or human faith you have, there are many things that are impossible for you to do.

It is impossible for man to save himself.

It is impossible for man to heal himself of incurable diseases.

It is impossible for man to bring himself out of the situation that the world tells us that we are in today. Every ecologist that you want to read after, every psychologist that you want to read after, and every sociologist that you want to hear give a lecture will tell you that we are doomed. "If we don't run out of food first, we are going to kill ourselves with pollution," the ecologists say. The sociologists say, "Well, if we keep going like we are, we are going to kill one another off, because everybody is mad at everybody else. Nobody can get along with anybody else." It goes on and on. Committees meet, legislators meet and they legislate, and when it is all said and done, they have accomplished nothing, and it is still impossible for man to get himself out of the situation that he finds himself in today. Why?

Because the devil has control of this thing. The Word of God said that he (Satan) is come to steal, and to kill, and to destroy.

You ask, "Well, what can we do?"

You need to get hold of possibility faith.

Unless you get hold of the *possibility faith* you cannot change your destiny; you can't change anything, and you are doomed.

There are some things that your natural human faith will accomplish, and you can do it because you believe in yourself. On the other hand, there are some things that you can believe all you want to, and you can do all you want to, but you will never be set free until you get hold of *possibility faith* from the Word of God.

Jesus said in Luke 18:27, "The things which are impossible with men are possible with God." And we read in Luke 1:37, "For with God nothing shall be impossible." Do you realize that when those two words *shall* and *be* are put together, they are the strongest words that we have in the English language? *It shall happen,* or *it shall be* is as strong as we can get in our language. With these two Scripture verses in mind, let's read Mark 11:22–24: "And Jesus answering saith unto them, Have faith in God. For verily I say unto you, That whosoever *shall say* unto this mountain, Be thou removed, and be thou cast into the sea; and *shall not doubt* in his heart, but *shall believe* that those things which he saith shall come to pass: he *shall have* whatsoever he saith. Therefore I say unto you, What things soever ye desire, when ye pray, believe that ye receive them, and *ye shall have* them." Jesus had walked by a fig tree on the day before, and in verse 14, He said, " . . . No man eat fruit of thee hereafter forever." Then in verse 21, Peter called this to Jesus' attention, and Jesus said in verse 22, " . . . Have faith in God." Some translations say, "Have the God kind of faith." The God kind of faith is the *possibility faith.* It is possible with the kind of faith that God has. *Possibility faith is a faith that believes in your heart and says with your mouth, and receives what you believe in your heart.*

I want you to thoroughly understand the kind of faith that we are talking about. When Jesus was talking about this kind of faith, He was saying, "Have this *possibility faith."* Or "Have the God kind of faith." He was talking about the kind of faith that God has always exercised. Read with me, back in the very first chapter in the Bible—Genesis 1:3, "**And God said,** Let there be light: and there was light." Verses 6-7 say, "**And God said,** Let there be a firmament in the midst of the waters, and let it divide the waters from the waters. And God made the firmament and divided the waters which were under the firmament from the waters which were above the firmament: and it was so." Look down at verse 9: "**And God said,** Let the waters under the heaven be gathered together unto one place and let dry land appear: and it was so." Read verse 14: "**And God said,** Let there be lights in the firmament of the heaven to divide. . . ." And then He divided day and night, and it says at the close of verse 15, " . . . and it was so." We go on down to verse 20, and it says, "**And God said,** Let the waters bring forth abundantly the moving creature that hath life, and fowl that may fly above the earth in the open firmament of heaven." And He says that it was good. It was done. I want you to notice that in verse 24, the Word says, "**And God said,** Let the earth bring forth the living creature after his kind, cattle, and creeping thing, and beast of the earth after his kind: and it was so." Can you see that this first chapter of the Word of God is a demonstration of that *God kind of possibility faith?* That *possibility faith* is the kind of faith that speaks and it is so. It said, "God spoke, and it was so."

Christian, I want you to realize this: you and I have become the sons of God. You and I are members of the family of God, and we have become joint-heirs with Jesus

Christ. I want you to realize that after having become a member of the family of God, you have been adopted into that family (through salvation), and you have been given that same kind of *possibility faith* that God has, because He is your Father. You can speak and it shall be so! Praise God. I want you to realize that it is up to you to exercise your own *possibility faith* in order to receive what you want from God.

You may know all about your *possibility faith,* and you may talk about it. You can even tell others how to use their *possibility faith,* and yet fail to receive yourself. Some time ago, I heard an individual saying to someone else, "Now, here's what you do. You begin to believe God. The Word of God says, 'My God shall supply all of your (my) needs according to His riches in glory. . . .'" He went on and told them what to do. "Now you have to believe it, confess that it is so, and it will happen." You know that guy told the individual how to receive financial help, and that person started living in the financial prosperity that he should.

Later, someone walked up to this same guy who had been doing all of the teaching and said, "Hey, everybody is getting together and going out to eat."

That same fellow said, "I can't go. I don't have the money." He had just told his friend how to be set free, and then he turned around and said, "I don't have the money. I can't go." You see, he knew the principles of *possibility faith,* and he could tell somebody else how to use it, but he wasn't living in the blessing of it himself. It had never gone beyond his head (intellect). It had never gotten into his heart (spirit).

The Bible says that nothing is impossible with God. People will say, "Oh praise God! Nothing is impossible with God." They will talk about this *possibility faith*; then the next thing you know, they will be wringing their hands and crying. "Oh yeah, Brother Hagin, I want to tell you I want that *possibility faith* so much. I have been just hoping and praying that I will get it." They may as well start singing the *Camptown Races—do-dah, do-dah, do-dah day*, because that is all the good it is going to get them—to pray for faith.

This possibility faith, the kind of faith that speaks and it is so, will come to you only one way. Romans 10:17 says, "So then faith cometh by hearing and hearing and hearing and hearing and hearing and hearing by the Word of God" (Author's paraphrase). The Word of God has much to say about hearing. In fact, all through the New Testament you will find these words penned: "He that hath an ear, let him hear what the Spirit is saying." Well, we all have ears.

God is trying to get something over to His people. He wants you to know that it is not enough to hear it with your two physical ears: It's not enough just to let it go into your two ear canals: It's not enough to let that sound vibrate off of the eardrums and all the little particles down in your ear where you are able to understand and to hear. He is saying, "You have to get it, or hear it with the spirit, way down on the inside." When many people watch television, and the commercial comes on, they flip a little switch mentally and cut out the sound for about 30 to 60 seconds. When the program slips back on the screen and they hear the theme music, they flip the mental switch back on and they are tuned right back to the program that they were watching. They never even heard the commercial. Some people act the same way with the things of God. They will sit in the house of God, listen to good singing, and then jump up and praise God. They will clap their hands and sing and say, "Oh, praise God! Hallelujah! Oh, isn't this great?" But the moment the Word starts coming forth they flip a switch, mentally speaking, and they don't hear the Word. Then when the end of the service comes, and they start playing the music and singing, they flip their mental switch on again and they get all excited. I want to tell you: that's good and I like that. I'm not against somebody getting excited for God occasionally, but don't flip the switch off when the man starts to deliver the Word of God—that's the most important part.

You can live without all that inspiration, and all that good feeling, but you cannot live without knowing the real principles of this *possibility faith*.

Exercise your possibility faith.

The Word of God says that it is impossible for you to please God if you don't have this *possibility faith*. I didn't say it. Another fellow by the name of Hagin didn't say it. Many people get the idea that this faith message is Hagin's message. NO! It is not Hagin's message. It is God's message to His children. It just so happens that my father was the one man that I know who had the *guts* (pardon that Texas

8

talk), and the daring to stand in the face of every obstacle and say, "Faith in God works!" when it wasn't popular.

You will find yourself in a similar situation when you start exercising this *possibility faith*. People will look strangely at you as if they think that you fell *out of a well*, or fell *up the stairs*. They will look at you and say, "Hey! Wait a minute. Where are you coming from anyway?"

Don't let it bother you. Just simply believe what God says and exercise your *possibility faith* in the face of every contradicting circumstance, and when you do this, it shall be so!

I can preach to you and teach you all that I know about faith. You can read and study all you want to about faith. You can open yourself up like a sponge. Then when you come to the last page of this book and put it down, you should be so full of faith and the power of God that you will begin to receive all the good things. But—do you know many of you who read this book will be like a sponge? You will be saturated with the facts concerning *possibility faith*. But the minute you get where there is unbelief, and the circumstances of life hit you, it will be like a steam roller rolling over you. When you put a sponge down that is full of water and a steam roller rolls over it and you pick it up again, there is no water left in it. When the steam rollers of circumstances, disease, and financial peril try to roll right over the top of you, you are going to have to keep that *possibility faith* turned on, and keep talking it. It won't be long until—as you keep speaking it—that steam roller will stop, turn course, and go another direction.

Because of who you are in Christ who lives inside you, you have *possibility faith*. But unless you learn how to use it, you will be run over like the steam roller runs over the sponge, or a rock, or anything else that gets in its way. You have to learn to use this possibility faith. It won't work by itself.

A lot of Christians think that it's like this: you will hear them say, "Well, if God wants me to have it I'll get it sometime. I am going to get my healing one of these days." They will say, "Brother Hagin, I want to tell you, I am going to get my healing one of these days. I am going to get up out of this bed. I am going to walk out of this wheelchair. Oh, one of these days I'm gonna have me one of those big nice houses. . . . " Well, that has been three years ago, and they are still talking, and *I ain't seen nothing yet* (pardon that Texas colloquialism)! I haven't seen anything yet! There isn't any manifestation whatsoever.

I have also had others come up to me and say, "Brother Hagin, the Word of God says, 'This is my time.' The Word of God says, 'This is my day.'" And I have seen them walk out of wheelchairs. Others have said, "Brother Hagin, the next time you see me, I am going to be driving new wheels, because the Word of God says, 'This is my day.'" And they were too!

What's the difference?

Well, one person was just talking—using head faith, and the other was making a confession based on the Word of God—using *possibility faith*.

If you say, "Oh, I claimed something. I put my faith on that and nothing happened." It is because you are not using that *possibility faith* correctly.

There are three categories of faith people.

I have been around this thing all of my life. I was born with the faith message. I have seen it and I have grown up with it. I have seen faith work from the beginning to the end. I am not bragging on myself, but I can talk with people for five minutes about faith and the things of God, and I can categorize them. Faith people come under three categories.

1. **The excited faith people:** These are the ones who have been where the Word has been preached. They are caught up with the inspiration of the moment and everybody is all excited, "Whoo! Brother. . . . " They have excited possibility faith. They never recognize the true facts. They won't even acknowledge the facts. These excited faith people will be excited the next time you see them, but they won't be getting anything. They run into the ditch on the left side of the road.

2. **The undecided people:** They say, "The Bible says I'm healed, but I don't know. I still hurt. I guess I'm not healed." They make a faith confession one time, and they are snared by their own words the next. They lean to their own understanding. Proverbs 3:5 says, " . . . lean not to your own understanding."

They run into the ditch on the right side of the road. They acknowledge the facts too much.

3. **The positive confession people:** These are the people who use their possibility faith. They keep in the middle of the road. A man in the middle of the road will say, "Bless God, the books say that we are *in the red.* My body says that it hurts. That is a fact: I can't deny that. But armed with the greater facts of God's Word, I make my confession on the Word of God. The Word of God says, 'All of my needs are met!' And I confess that the ledger book will total up *in the black.* My Bible says that, 'By His stripes I am healed!' and when all is said and done the pain will be gone. The disease will be gone, and I shall be well." This individual recognizes that the problem exists, but he takes his *possibility faith* and puts it on his needs, and he gets results.

I am not trying to put anybody down. I just want people to wake up. Reader—Christian, if you are going to get anything from God, you have to get out of the category on the left, or get out of the category on the right, and get into the middle of the road. You see, there are too many people who take the faith message and they run off into the ditch.

Get your confession lined up with the Word of God, and exercise your *possibility faith.* You see, the individual who recognizes that a problem exists, and takes this *possibility faith* and puts it on the problem will see results.

A little side trip

A few years ago my father, Kenneth E. Hagin, came to me and said, "Son, God has led me to start a school for ministers." He said, "God wants you to run it, and be the head of it, and put it together."

I said, "I know it." My wife and I had known it for months. We were just waiting for Dad to get it from God.

Somebody may say, "Well, *how come* your Dad was so slow, if you had known it for months?"

Well, let me tell you—This is where a lot of people get into trouble. I'll just take you on a little side trip and show you something that can help you with your own family. Dad would have liked nothing better than for his own son to direct that school. He would have liked nothing better than for his own son (in the natural) to follow in his footsteps. But I want to tell you this: if God is not in it, it will mess up his ministry, my ministry, and everybody else's that would come in contact with us. So he was very slow in his decision because he wanted to be sure that it wasn't just from his head, as a natural father. He wanted to be sure that this was coming out of his heart (spirit), so he took his time in order to be sure that this was right.

We started the school and I walked in one day, and my secretary said, "Ken, here are the facts and the figures." I started to chuckle because I had already, in my mind, analyzed it, and I knew what it was already. She said, "Here it is. There are more disbursements than there is income.

There is going to be eight thousand more dollars disbursed this month than we've got income."

I took that piece of paper, and I walked through her office into my office. I pulled back my chair, sat down at my desk, and I took the ledger and laid it right down in front of me. I pushed back my chair a little bit and I said, "Now God, there it is. You can read it. I don't have to tell you what it is. You know: there it is. The figures say that we have eight thousand more dollars to disburse than we have income coming in this month. Now, Heavenly Father, there are the facts. They exist. They are there in black and white and red. They are there."

In case you don't know anything about bookkeeping, I had white paper, black figures, and then when I looked down at the bottom there was a red figure with red brackets around it! That meant that I didn't have that much money in the account! I looked up and I said, "All right God, there it is. But taking the greater facts of this Word of God that I have been preaching and teaching, I say with my mouth, according to the Word of God, 'When this month is over, we will have paid every bill, and still have in the bank what it says that we have right now. We are going to pay all the bills and even pay the extra eight thousand dollars and still have in the bank what we have now.'"

Somebody said, "That's a big bite to bite off!"

Yeah, it was for me. But I was putting my *possibility faith* on it. I picked up the ledger and took it back to her office, and threw it down on her desk as I said, "It's taken care of. Put it in the file drawer."

Now, all month long, every time I unlocked the door and walked through her office, I had to walk right beside that file cabinet that had the ledger in it—that had everything in it! I knew that all I had to do was to open that drawer, and I could look and see how much money was coming in. It was in there! It was written down! I could know exactly how much was coming in every day. I would unlock the door and as I walked by that file cabinet, the devil would slow me down, and say, "Hey, why don't you just take a look? Why don't you just take a peek, then you will know for sure?"

I said, "Mr. Devil, I have already taken care of the problem. I don't have to peek to see if it's coming in. I know it's coming, because possibility faith speaks and it happens!"

God said, "Let there be. . . . " and it was. Jesus said to the fig tree, "Dry up. . . . " and it did. Once you get hold of this principle, and learn to live with it, you will see some things change in your life. So—I walked right into my office, picked up my books, and went to class, and I taught. Sometimes, I wished that I had moved that file cabinet, but it wouldn't have done any good. Satan would still have harassed me. I know I had to walk by that thing twenty or thirty times a day, and every time I walked by, the devil would jump upon my shoulder and start hollering. And I would say, "According to the Word of God, it's met."

It was the end of the month, and I knew that my secretary was balancing the books. I knew she was doing the monthly report. I was sitting in my office taking care of business when I heard somebody at the door, and there she stood with a big smile on her face. She laid the report down, but I didn't have to look at it to know. You see, I took care of that situation back at the first of the month. In fact, it was one of those short months (February). I didn't even pick it up! I began to praise God. "I thank you, Jesus!" I said to the devil, "You see, Mr. Devil, I told you. Twenty-eight days ago, I told you that this thing was already taken care of. You tried to harass me. Now I am going to pick up these papers and just see how much excess the Lord has thrown in."

We had paid every bill that there was to pay, and had more in the bank than we had when we started the month!

Now, I want to tell you something: If just one time I had opened that drawer, whether I even looked at the book or not, if I had stopped myself short of looking in the book: if one time, I had gone back on my faith and just reached down and opened that drawer, I could have forgotten the whole thing. I would have given in to the devil, and my *possibility faith* would have been gone. *Possibility faith* has to be of your heart, and you have to exercise it.

If you are not receiving, it is because you are not putting your faith that you know—the faith that you have in your heart—into action. You are not actually believing for your-self. You are wanting somebody else to believe for you.

Don't stay in the spiritual nursery.

God compares spiritual growth with physical growth. And there are some Christians who are still in the spiritual nursery when they should already be in the first or second grade. They are supposed to be growing up, but they are still in the nursery. I have a son, Craig, who (at the time of this writing) is eight years old. I also have a four year old daughter, Denise. If Denise says, "Daddy, I want some milk," I will get up and go get her a glass of milk, because she can't handle a big gallon of milk, and she can't reach the glasses in the cabinet yet. But if Craig comes in and says, "Daddy, I'm thirsty. I want something to drink," I will say, "Get it yourself." You see, I expect him to do something on his own. It is morally wrong for me to wait on him hand and foot.

That is what is the matter with a lot of young people today. They have been waited on hand and foot. When they are old enough to take responsibility, they don't know how because they have been given everything. I tell my son, "You know where it is. Go get it yourself "

Now this is what God is saying to some of us today. "Son, daughter, I have taken care of you all I can. It is time that you start taking care of yourself. It's time that you start doing something on your own. It's time that you start exercising your own possibility faith and receive for yourself."

I just told you how. I just told you that you have it. I just told you that you have to believe it in your heart, and not in your head. Now, don't say it because I told you to. It doesn't work that way. You do it because you really believe it in your heart.

It is time that you receive (from God today) what you want. And you do this by acting on it in true faith, and using your *possibility faith*.

Are you ready? Confess the Word of God.

The Word of God says, "By His stripes I am healed."

The Word of God says, "According to His riches in glory, all of my needs are met."

The Word of God says, "Greater is He that is in me than he that is in the world." So the greater one lives in me. He is greater than any habit. He's greater than any financial difficulty. He's greater than any thing that I can name.

The Word of God says, "I am more than a conqueror in Christ Jesus."

If you will begin to quote what the Word of God says, and begin to use your *possibility faith,* you will begin to walk along life's road holding the hand of Jesus, and singing Victory in Jesus: Standing on the Promises, I cannot fall when the howling storms of doubt and fear assail. By the living Word of God I shall prevail: Standing on the promises, I've got victory over all! Hallelujah to Jesus! If you will take your *possibility faith* and begin to exercise it according to the Word of God, you can have what you want from God today.

CHAPTER 2

Possibility Faith:
You Have It

The Word of God says, "And He said, The things which are impossible with men are possible with God" (Luke 18:27). This is Jesus talking, and I want you to notice that He hasn't qualified that statement. He didn't say that *certain things* are impossible with men that are possible with God. He said, " . . . **the things** which are impossible with men are possible with God." **Things.** THINGS. Things mean *anything that you want to put under that category.* This book is a *thing.* A suit of clothes is a *thing.* A circumstance in life is a *thing* that gets in your way and keeps you from receiving. Read it again: " . . . *the things* which are impossible with men are possible with God." He is talking about an impossibility becoming a possibility. How can this happen?

Through faith—that one word FAITH—impossibilities become possibilities. According to Webster's dictionary, one of the definitions under the word *faith* is this: *Faith is an unquestionable trust in God, or an unquestionable belief in the things of God.*

I have had people come to me and say, "Brother Hagin, I would like to ask you a question. Now, don't get me wrong. I believe with all of my heart, and I have faith, but I'd like to ask you. . . . " Invariably they ask a question that proves to me that they do not believe. If they believed, they wouldn't be asking the question. It is not a sin to *not* believe if you don't understand. You cannot believe if you don't have knowledge of the Word of God. If you find yourself in a situation where you are not quite understanding what someone is saying (teaching), don't be afraid to acknowledge the fact. Say, "Look, I have faith, but I don't understand what you are saying, and I want it explained to me so I can believe."

Too many people are afraid that somebody is going to condemn them. And they have a reason for this.

We, who are strong in faith have gone against what Paul taught in the New Testament. He has taught us to *not condemn* those who are *not as strong* in faith as we are. We have so put people down to where they are even afraid to talk to us, and ask us about some things, so that they can have strong faith. They can't believe beyond their actual knowledge of the Word of God.

I would like for everybody to be able to believe God like I can. I'm not putting any flowers on my shoulders. I am simply telling you a fact that I have learned over a period of years. In our home believing God was a way of life. I don't know anything else. If everybody could believe like some can, that is, be as strong in faith as many of us, there would be no need to even teach on it. What I am saying is: Don't *put people down* or put them under condemnation because they do not have as strong faith as you. People have been put under so much condemnation, for asking a simple question concerning faith, that now they are afraid to ask. And no wonder: We jump right in the middle of them with all four feet, and start clawing and scratching.

We should be saying: "Hey, look, I once had the same problem that you are having. I can take you to the Word and show you the answer." If we would do that, we would find more people moving the impossibilities out of their lives.

We read in Mark 11:22-24, "And Jesus answering saith unto them, Have faith in God. For verily I say unto you, That whosoever shall say unto this mountain, Be thou removed, and be thou cast into the sea; and shall not doubt in his heart, but shall believe that those things which he saith shall come to pass; he shall have whatsoever he saith. Therefore I say unto you, What things soever ye desire, when ye pray, believe that ye receive them, and ye shall have them."

Now, contrary to some people's belief, Kenneth E. Hagin did not write the above Scripture passage! He happens to be my father, and I know that he didn't write it. So, if you hear somebody saying that, you can tell them that you heard it from his son: he did not write Mark 11:22-24!

I believe that he does have some forty to sixty messages from those Scripture verses, that he preaches. One day a guy asked him, "Reckon you'll ever run out of sermons on those verses of Scripture?"

Dad said, "NO! Because we've never learned all there is to learn about faith and confession and believing God."

The day that we learn all there is about believing God is the day that we will reach perfection. And that is the day that Jesus Christ will return to this earth. That is when, according to Ephesians, the saints will come into the maturity of perfection. Then, we won't have to have any more faith teaching. We will know all that there is to know about it.

Jesus told us in the above Scripture passage, "Have faith in God, or have the God kind of faith." Impossibilities can become possibilities if you have the God kind of faith. What is the God kind of faith?

In chapter one of this book, we went back to the very first chapter of the Bible and saw how God exercised His God kind of faith—His possibility faith, and brought the world into existence. "And God said, Let there be . . . firmament, light, and waters." We read also in verse 26 of the book of Genesis, "And God said, Let us make man in our image, after our likeness. . . . " It tells how God created man. He used His God kind of faith—possibility faith—and spoke the worlds into existence. You can trace this from the Old Testament to the New Testament, where it talks about Christ in John 1:3, "All things were made by him; and without him was not any thing made that was made." And in Hebrews 11:3, we read, "Through faith we understand that the worlds were framed by the Word of God, so that things which are seen were not made of things which do appear."

You remember that Jesus told the disciples, as they talked about the incident of the fig tree, to have faith in God, or have the God kind of faith. He told them something else over in Matthew 17:20. The disciples were asking Jesus why they couldn't cure the lunatic. And these are Jesus' words: " . . . Because of your unbelief: for verily I say unto you, If ye have faith as a grain of mustard seed, ye shall say unto this mountain, Remove hence to yonder place; and it shall remove; and nothing shall be impossible unto you." Do you see how these two Scripture passages tie together? "Have the God kind of faith:" and, "Nothing shall be impossible unto you." He is saying the same thing in both Scripture passages: "Man's impossibility becomes God's possibility because of the faith of God." That kind of faith in God is the kind of faith that you and I have; that we can say with our mouths and expect results.

Confess what the Word of God says.

It is most important for you to know that when you say something with your mouth you have to make your confession based upon the Word of God, and believe it in your heart. You can make confessions all day long, but if you are not making your confession based upon the Word of God— in line with the Word of God, and believing it in your heart, you will never get a thing.

People have so pushed faith on to those who are sick, and have hounded them so much until they have gotten those people making faith confessions when they don't really believe it in their hearts. To get the person off of their backs they will make a confession of faith, and nothing happens. The one who hounded that one into making a faith confession, when he wasn't ready, has given Satan an avenue to start working and throwing his seeds of doubt and unbelief all over the place, and he has himself a good little carnival in that person's life.

Don't force people into making a confession of faith. If you see that they aren't ready to make a confession of faith, keep feeding them the Word. Keep feeding them good faith tapes about people who have received. If you will feed them enough of the Word of God, they will receive the God kind of faith, and then they will be ready to make a confession of their own, and to receive for themselves.

They have faith already, because it says in the Word of God that you are saved through faith, and that not of your-selves. It is the gift of God. (See Ephesians 2:8.)

One faith: different levels.

God has only one kind of faith, and that same faith that was given to you when you were saved is the same faith that you use to create possibility where man says that it is impossible. I wish to emphasize this: we don't have one kind of faith to be saved, one kind of faith to receive the Holy Spirit, one kind of faith to receive our healing, and another kind of faith to live for Christ. It is all one faith. **One faith.** That one faith will do the job for all our needs.

If you were going to work with heavy equipment, and you were going to do an extra heavy job, you would need heavier equipment than you would need for a smaller job. You can pull a certain kind of load with a certain kind of engine, but if you are going to pull a heavy load over the Rockies, you are going to need a more powerful engine in that diesel truck, than you would need for the flatlands in West Texas. Out there in the wheat fields you can see for a hundred miles, and there isn't anything between you and the north pole but a barbed wire fence! You don't need all that power because you don't have any hills to climb. If you put the same amount of weight on a truck that you are going to take up into the mountains, it won't work because it isn't geared for the job. You will need a heavier truck with more power in the engine to climb the mountain. On the other hand you can use the larger truck with the heavier engine both places, then you will only need one piece of equipment to do both jobs.

In the area of faith, there is only one engine—the God kind of faith, and it does all the jobs for us, both in the mountains and on the plains. There is only one kind of faith, *but there are different levels of faith.*

Some people will say that there are different kinds of faith. No. there are not different kinds of faith, but there are different levels of faith. They will quote the Scriptures that tell you of the different levels of faith, and then they call them, "different kinds of faith." They are using the wrong terminology.

Some will say, "Well, I can't be healed because you know that I don't have that kind of strong faith. Now, only a few people have that strong faith that he talks about." No: strong faith is not a different kind of faith. It is a different level of faith.

The reason some people have strong faith is because they have taken the Word of God, and they have listened, and listened, and listened, and listened again. "Faith cometh by hearing and hearing by the Word of God." Sometimes, we would be better off to take all the punctuation marks out of the Scriptures, because they were not in there originally: neither were the chapter divisions or verses. In fact, the people who put the Bible together have actually done an injustice to us in 1 Corinthians 13; 14; and 15. They divided it up when it should have been *all one discourse,* and taken into context together. The same thing was done with Romans 10:17. It reads, "So then faith cometh by hearing, and hearing by the word of God." If you take the punctuation marks out, it reads like this, and you can see that it is a continual thing: "So then faith cometh by hearing and hearing by the word of God." You get people to hear the Word of God, and they get faith by hearing and hearing and hearing and hearing the Word of God.

Don't get them to make confessions out of their heads and not out of their hearts. When they do this nothing is going to happen. The impossibility situation remains impossible, and they get into a quandary over it, and they don't know what to do. Just keep feeding them the Word. They need to listen to faith testimonies. They need to hear the Word and their faith will grow. Then they will make their own confessions out of their hearts and not out of their heads.

One example of feeding people the Word so they can make the right confession.

Some good examples of man's impossibility, and God's possibility are recorded in the books of Dr. Lilian B. Yeomans, M.D.[1] Dr. Yeomans' books were out of print for a number of years, and my father thought so much of those books that he sent my brother-in-law to the Gospel Publishing House in Springfield, Missouri to see if we could either buy the copyrights or have them to republish them. They republished them and they are some of the best faith books that you can read.

Dr. Yeomans for a large part of her life was a regular medical doctor. She became addicted to cocaine and other narcotics, and of course any time a physician does this, he or she loses his or her license to practice medicine. Then— she was saved, delivered, and set free. She was healed by the power of God, and for the rest of her life, instead of practicing physical medicine, Dr. Yeomans practiced divine medicine.

For a number of years Dr. Yeomans lived in Southern California, and she taught divine healing in two colleges:

L.I.F.E. Bible College, and the Southern California Bible College. She taught at one college in the morning, and at the other in the afternoon.

Dad had been reading some of Dr. Yeomans' books, and he happened to be talking (about Dr. Yeomans) to some of the men who had been in her classes. One fellow said this to Dad: "One time, when I was working the midnight shift, and going to Bible school in the daytime, I went up to her and said, 'Dr. Yeomans, would you pray for my cold?' She looked at me and said, 'Well, if it's your cold it won't do any good to pray about it.' I said, 'Oh, would you pray and agree with me about the devil's cold? And she said, 'Sure!'"

Dr. Yeomans taught that this was the way that you accepted the package (when you called it "my cold"). You hear these same teachings today.

Dr. Yeomans inherited a mansion somewhere in Southern California, and she turned it into a home where people could go when they had terminal diseases. They came there in ambulances. Of course, since she had been a medical physician for all of those years, she had not lost her knowledge. Dr. Yeomans said that as she would begin to examine some of those patients, if she had still been practicing medicine, she would have begun to give them shots immediately to stimulate them. But, of course she wasn't practicing medicine, so she and her sister would take them upstairs and begin to read them the Word of God. There was a woman who had tuberculosis (TB). They read to her from Galatians 3:13; about Christ redeeming her (us) from the curse of the law. Then they would go back to Deuteronomy 28, and read about the curses of the law. Right there in verse 22 it talks about consumption. That is what they called tuberculosis back then. Then, along with those two Scripture passages they would read other verses on faith and healing. Over and over they read them to that lady for about a three day period (I believe it was).

One day, Dr. Yeomans' sister had just left the room to go downstairs to help prepare the food, and to take it back upstairs to the patients, and suddenly they heard someone hit the floor. Remember: they had deathly ill people up there, and none of them were strong enough to get out of bed. But all of a sudden they heard somebody hit that floor, and she began to dance and holler. Of course they ran to see what was happening, and about that time a lady came sweeping down that spiral staircase!

"Sister Yeomans! Sister Yeomans! Did you know that I've been healed of TB? Did you know that Christ died and He took the stripes upon His back, and I don't have TB; anymore?" She was shouting and praising the Lord!

You see, the faith that comes by hearing and hearing and hearing the Word of God had gotten into her heart, and when enough of that faith had been pumped in there, she began to realize that. And she jumped up and began to do something herself. That is when the impossibility became possibility!

We need to give people the Word of God so that their faith will come up to the level to receive. We make a mistake when we try to get them to move the mountains out of the way when they aren't even ready to speak to the molehills.

In case you do not know about moles and molehills, I will tell you! Down where I came from (Texas), they have small animals called "moles." They burrow long tunnels under the ground, and when they come up to the surface of the ground they leave a small hill about six inches high. You can kick that little hill over with your foot. Some people have molehill faith, and they take that level of faith and try to move Mount Everest with it. Now, I can kick over a molehill, but I am not about to go over there and try to kick over Mount Everest!

Build up your level of faith.

If your faith is not up to the level in the spiritual world to where you can turn impossibilities into possibilities, you need to exercise it and build it up to that level. Some people have said to me, "Brother Hagin, that's the *kind of faith* that I want. I have been praying that God will help me to have that *kind of faith*. I have prayed and fasted for the last three days before you got here, so that when you came you would lay your hands on me, and I would get that *kind of faith*."

I have looked at them, and I have just wanted to shake them a little bit and say, "Didn't you hear what I said tonight?" Of course I can't do that. But you know they have just sat there where the Word of God was being delivered, and they did not hear. They still believe that there are different kinds of faith.

We make the mistake of seeing people in the services, and just because we got hold of the message we assume that they received it too. We go to them and talk about all of this faith, and they do not understand. They have been in the same services that we were in, but they were only there with their physical bodies. They have not heard.

The Word of God says this, over and over again, and I say it again and again, "He that hath ears let him hear." Or "He that hath an ear, let him hear." (Matthew 11:15; Mark 4:9,23; 7:16; Luke 8:8; 14:35; Revelation 2:7, 11, 17, 29; 3:6, 13, 22; 13:9)

He isn't talking about the physical ears: He is talking about the spiritual ear. Let it get through the spiritual ears down on the inside.

Many people go to church and their bodies are there, but they are out working on the car, or planning a vacation, or doing all kinds of things. This happened to me once when I was in Bible School.

The teacher threw a pop-quiz at us, and I didn't do so very good in spite of the fact that I usually made pretty good grades. He called me in and said, "Ken, what's the matter with you? You have never made a grade like this before."

I said, "Aw, it's my fault."

He said, "But you have been in class every day."

"Yeah," I answered, "my body has been in class, but my head hasn't. I have been designing football plays, and trying to figure out what we can do to beat the Junior College." We were going to play the junior college for the championship, and my body had been in class, but my mind and my spirit had been playing football. Therefore I didn't learn what the teacher had been teaching, and when he wanted the answers back on a sheet of paper, I couldn't give them to him.

That is what happens to us when we haven't been hearing the Word and exercising our faith. We come up against an impossible situation and we can do nothing about it, because our faith isn't up to the level that we can change that impossibility to possibility. A doctor may say, "I'm sorry, but you have a certain disease, and we can do nothing for you."

If that happens to you, that is a sad indictment against either you, or your preacher. One of two things has happened. Either the man is not preaching the Word, or you are not hearing it. I am sorry to say that about 80 percent of the time the person who is doing the preaching or teaching to you has not been preaching or teaching the true Word of God, and your faith could not grow.

I have felt sorry for people who haven't heard the Word, and I have said, "How can they hear except a preacher preach the Word to them?" Then I get back to this point and say, "Well, bless God, they have the Word of God, and the Spirit of God. They can find out for themselves if they will just get into the Word. Therefore the indictment lies at both doors: the preacher's, or teacher's fault for not giving out the true Word of God, and the Christian's fault for not getting into the Word and studying for himself (or herself). The fact remains that when the Word of God is given, and when faith comes into your heart, and you begin to let it grow, those impossible situations become possible.

Once I was standing in the corridor of a hospital, and a doctor came out of the intensive care ward. He gathered a family around him and said to me, "Preacher, come on over here. I've got sad news for this family."

"Ok. Ok." I said as I walked over there.

The doctor looked at them and said, "I'm sorry, we have done all we can do. It's just a matter of time."

The family looked at him, and didn't blink an eye: nobody went into hysterics, or began to scream and holler.

He called me over to one side and said, "Did they hear what I said?"

"Yes, Doctor, they heard what you said," I answered.

"Did they understand?"

"Sure," I replied. "But you see, we are not looking to man. Our faith is not in what man can do. Our faith is in what God can do, and God says *when it's impossible with man it is possible with God.*"

"Oh, one of them!" the doctor said as he walked off. But today that individual is alive because we would not allow an impossible situation to remain.

Take your vitamins.

Many good Christians have faith, but they have never put it to work in their lives. Thereby they are imprisoned by impossibilities, when they hold the key to the door that will unlock the prison cell of impossibility, and tear all of the bars asunder, and make it a possible situation; simply by quoting the Word of God.

Faith is like vitamin C: It cannot be stored for a rainy day. You have to take vitamin C into your body every day. If you don't, you will find yourself getting weak, and physical things won't work properly. The same thing is true concerning spiritual things. You have to take the Word of God, over, and over, and over again, to keep your faith strong. You have to exercise that faith to keep it at a possibility level just as you exercise the muscles in your body to keep them at a level to lift weights.

Perhaps you have seen the huge man from Russia on television. He lifts approximately 580 pounds over his head. Do you think that he walked into that? No! He gets up every morning, walks into the gym, and goes to work. He does a few exercises to warm up and to get his muscles loose, then he picks up a few weights and lifts them; then he adds a little more weight until he builds up to that amount of weight. He will then add a little extra to see if he can lift that. That is the way that he pushes and builds his muscles larger. He is on a strenuous program to do that every day. If he doesn't do so, he cannot be ready for the contest. Even when he is in a contest he will warm up in the back room before going out on the stage. Sometimes he will do this for hours—to keep from pulling a muscle.

Christian, you need to begin to take the Word of God and to live with it daily, and work with it. If nothing else, have your time of prayer and study before you leave your house in the morning. Take one Scripture verse and mull it over in your mind all day long. Quote it every time you think about it. If you are running a machine, or you are on an assembly line job, you can meditate on the Word. I was on an assembly line job when I went to Bible school. I did the same thing over and over for eight hours. I would take what we called "pills," and pre-heat them in something similar to a microwave oven, dump them in a mold, hit the control to close the mold, and wait until the mold released. Then I would take an air hose and give them a shot of air, and presto! plastic plates. I would pack them up, take some more plastic pills, put them in the mold, and on, and on! I could stand there and sleep, because I was doing the same thing over, and over, and over again. As I worked that job, from midnight until 7:00 the next morning, I could quote Scriptures, and still meet my quota! I would just begin to think—"Now faith is . . . Now faith is . . . Have the God kind of faith . . . Have the God kind of faith. . . . " I would say, "Now the God kind of faith says something. What is it saying?" Before I knew it I had piled those dishes HIGH! as I mulled over the Word of God.

The boss came by and said, "Man! Hagin, you are ahead of schedule!" You see, I was doing my job, but my mind was thinking on the things of God.

If you want to be a person who speaks and something happens, then you are going to have to keep yourself full of faith. Remember over in the Book of Acts, when they picked out those seven deacons to work in the church. It says that Stephen was a man, full of faith. Some pretty impossible situations happened in Stephen's life. When the Libertines, the Cyrenians, the Alexandrians, and others were persecuting him, Stephen had the God kind of faith. He knew that God was with him, and being full of the faith of God, Stephen preached the Word of God from Abraham to Jesus with boldness. Then, he showed the love of God as he asked Him to forgive them for stoning him to death. He changed man's impossibility to God's possibility, and he saw the heavens open, and Jesus standing at the right hand of God. A young man named "Saul," who held the coats of the ones who martyred Stephen, heard that message, and little did he know that very soon—man's impossibility would become God's possibility because the persecutor Saul would soon become the apostle Paul. He was going to meet Jesus on the road to Damascus.

Phillip was one of the seven, and also a man, full of faith. Phillip obeyed the Lord without question when he was told to go into the desert Gaza at noontime. He literally ran to do the Spirit's bidding, and he led the Ethiopian eunuch to the Lord. After he baptized the new Christian,

Phillip was translated from Gaza to Azotus. That was a 25-mile ride! Man's impossibility became God's possibility.

Faith worketh by love. Faith worketh by love.

Once, as I was teaching about this same subject, the Lord kept impressing me, way down on the inside of me—in my spirit. And I kept hearing these words over, and over, and over again. These are His Words, and I believe that He wants you to receive them.

"Impossibilities will only become possibilities when faith works with love—when faith works with love.

Faith will work, if you will love. Faith will move the mountain, if you will allow the bitterness to flow from your life. Faith will work for you in the area of prosperity, if you will turn loose of the bitterness and resentfulness that is in your heart. Faith will work for you, if you will really—only believe me, and allow my love to demonstrate Himself in you. You will see a great change.

Oh. Oh. Oh. Some of these things are very deep within your heart, and only if you will look deep will you see that you are still holding something against certain individuals, and you must release it before this faith that you have released with your mouth will ever work for you, because you are holding a grudge. Remember—Faith worketh by love, saith the Lord."

Praise God! I want to show you something else here, concerning working or changing impossibilities into possible situations. Several years ago, there was a man who was a state overseer of a certain denomination, and a close friend of ours. He passed on to his reward after living out his life down here. It was time to go, and he went home to the Lord without sickness or disease. Dad went over to talk with the widow, who was very distraught. He began to give her the Word: "To die is gain: To go on to be with Christ is far better. . . . "

He then told her, "Sure, you are going to feel the loss, but actually when you keep saying, 'Oh, what are we going to do without him? you are being selfish. That is not in line with the Word of God. The Word teaches that when somebody dies in Christ—goes to sleep in the Lord, it is a beautiful thing. Sure you will miss him, physically, but he is far better off than we are."

After Dad talked to her, she began to say, "Well, praise God, that's right. He did a great work for God down here, and now, God has let him go home. God didn't call him home, but he lived out his time, and he went on home. He is with the Lord. He is far better off. Praise the Lord."

The lady was all smiles, and then here came a carload of preachers and their wives. By the time they hit the porch they were crying, "Oh, what are we going to do? We just can't make it without him."

Dad said that he stood there and thought, "Well, who is their trust in? The state overseer who was really a man of God, or is it in God?"

The Word of God teaches that the body is decaying day by day—whether it gets sick or not. But it will decay a whole lot faster if it is sick. The inner man is renewed, but the body has not been redeemed yet. Paul says in Romans 8:22-23, "For we know that the whole creation groaneth and travaileth in pain together until now. And not only they, but ourselves also, which have the first fruits of the Spirit, even we ourselves groan within ourselves, waiting for the adoption, to wit, the redemption of our body." When Jesus comes back the body will be redeemed, but until then, the body keeps getting older. Paul said that the whole creation is groaning to be released, and to be redeemed. So—the body is going to die.

I remember when we stood around my 81-year-old Grandmother's (my dad's mother) bed, when she went to be with the Lord. As she drew her last breath, Dad let the Holy Spirit loose on the inside of him, and comforted all of us. From down on the inside of himself, Dad began to quote one Scripture after another. It was as if a tape recorder were turned on.

Once you learn how to let that Spirit down on the inside control, He will keep everything on an even keel. Sure, there is going to be a physical loss, and you will feel it, but if you will allow the Word of God to do its job, you can say, "Death, where is your sting?" There is no sting in death if you understand it, and know what it is all about—according to the Word of God.

Oh, there is a separation for a time, but thank God, there is no sting in death. When we cry and shed our tears, and I've done it too, we are really not shedding tears over them. We are shedding tears over our selfishness: because we don't want to lose them. And it's all right if you want to shed a few tears, God won't disown you.

Because people do not know the Word of God, the devil holds them in the prison of impossibilities, even though all things are possible to him that believeth. If we will allow the Word of God to work through us, with the love of God, then we can minister to people. We can tell them how to turn their impossibilities into possibilities, because we learn what the Word of God says.

The Word says: "Himself took our infirmities and bare our sicknesses, and by His stripes we are healed."

The Word says: "My God shall supply all of your needs according to His riches in glory. . . . "

The Word says . . . the Word says . . . the Word says. . . . Go get the Scripture that has to deal with your particular need, or your particular situation, and begin to say the Word. When Christ was faced with temptation, He said, "It is written." He spoke the Word to the devil.

When some of you come up against a little bit of temptation, you fall down and begin to cry, and pray, and fast. I believe in praying and crying—if you want to cry while you pray. And I believe in fasting, but it's not going to do you any good at that particular time when you are face to face with temptation. You are going to have to quote the Word in the face of that impossible situation, to make it a possible one.

You should spend your time praying and fasting in your regular prayer time, but when you are facing temptation, you should be ready—full of what the Word of God says, and overcome that impossibility by using that Word.

Jesus set the example. He prayed and fasted. In fact, before His greatest temptation came, He had just finished a fast. He was ready for the devil.

I will tell you this: When God tells you to go on some of the fasts that you go on, some of your greatest problems; some of your greatest temptations that you are ever going to have will hit you, just as you walk out the door. But because you've fasted, prayed, and been filled with His Word, you can use that same faith (God kind of faith) and turn that impossible situation into a possible situation by quoting the Word of God.

You have possibility faith—use it.

---

[1] Healing From Heaven; Balm of Gilead; Health and Healing; and The Great Physician: books by Dr. Lilian B. Yeomans, M.D. published by the Gospel Publishing House, Springfield, Missouri.

CHAPTER 3

Possibility Faith: It Can Grow

Impossibilities remain impossibilities because people's faith is of the head and not of the heart. Remember this: any time that you begin to believe God for an impossible situation and it doesn't work, you are not believing with your heart. You are only believing with your head, because when you believe with your heart, impossibilities become possibilities.

Check the receiving end.

The best way to check up on yourself if you are not receiving, is to check the receiving end. There is nothing wrong with the power source. The power station never shuts down. The trouble has to be at the receiving end. If the Word of God says it, then you will have to lay the facts where they are: accept those facts, and then accept the greater facts of God's Word, and go on to victory.

If you have been *hearing the Word of God with your spiritual ears* as you study with me, you now know that you have possibility faith: the God kind of faith. You may wish to review the following Scripture verses. Romans 12:3; Ephesians 2:8; Romans 10:17; and 2 Corinthians 4:13.

It is important for you to know that the measure of faith that God has given to every believer can be increased. As I told you before, there are not *different kinds* of faith. It is **all one faith**, but this faith can either be weak or strong: it can be less or great.

You can increase your measure of faith by doing three things.

1. *Feeding on the Word of God.* "So then faith cometh by hearing, and hearing by the word of God" (Romans 10:17).

2. *Exercising your faith.* Remember, in chapter two, we talked about the man exercising his muscles. He started out slowly and built his muscles up. You start out slowly to build your faith.

3. *Putting your faith into practice every day.* Believe God for something every day of your life, even if it is for something small. Most people don't use their faith every day. Many times, I tell people, "Believe God for something when you don't have to." This helps to keep your faith strong.

Sometimes, instead of taking money from my salary that I could use to buy something that I desire, I will use my faith to get it. That keeps my faith alive and strong. It keeps it built up so that when I face the impossible task I am at my best, and I am ready to conquer the impossibility with that possibility faith.

In this chapter, we are going to take a closer look at the real faith, Bible faith, scriptural faith, possibility faith, or the God kind of faith. That faith that turns impossible situations into possible situations is of the heart and not of the head. We will read again, Mark 11:23; "For verily I say unto you, That whosoever shall say unto this mountain, Be thou removed and be thou cast into the sea; and shall not doubt in his heart. . . . " And shall not doubt in his heart. And shall not doubt in his heart.

"Oh!" somebody said, "I'm beginning to see it! Yeah, that's the way you are saved. Romans 10:10 says, 'For with the heart man believeth. . . . '" For with the heart man believeth!—They will reread the above Scripture passages and say, "Well, the Word of God is crazy! How in the world can you believe with your heart? It's a muscle!"

You can't. You can't believe with your physical heart any more than you can believe with your eyes, your ears, your nose, your hand, your foot, or anything else that is part of your physical body. Paul is talking about the real man. If you will look into the Word of God you will find a couple of definitions of what God calls the spirit man. In 1 Peter 3:4, He calls the spirit man the "hidden man of the heart." In 2 Corinthians 4:16, He calls him, "the inward man." Therefore, God's definition of this spirit man (throughout the entire New Testament) is "a hidden man of the heart," or "an inward man," or the "inward man of the heart." In some places you will find that He just uses the word "heart."

Man contacts three areas of life. He contacts the physical, the mental (the mind, will, and the emotions), and the spiritual. You don't have to get into the Bible to find this out. Psychologists will tell you that. So—if God is a Spirit, and the Word of God says that He is, and if we are created in the image of God, and the Word of God says we are; then we are a spirit, we have a soul, and we live in a physical body. If you will begin to think about yourself in that way it will help your faith. It will help you to understand man, and it will help you to understand God. It will help you to understand many spiritual laws, because it will get you out of the realm of the physical, over into the realm of the spiritual. And that is where you have to be if you are going to understand God's laws and God's Word. You can't understand it with your head, you have to understand it with your heart. Proverbs 3:5 says, "Trust in the Lord with all thine heart; and lean not to thine own understanding." Here is that word "heart" again. I would like to read the same Scripture verse like this: "Trust in the Lord with all of your spirit and might, and lean not to your head" (Author's paraphrase). That doesn't do any harm to the Word of God. It just brings it down into a language that we can better understand.

Your own understanding comes from the physical and mental senses. Your faith must not be based on anything physical. This impossibility moving faith has to be based upon God's Word. It is not how you feel, but it is what the Word of God says about it. Your possibility faith is not in feelings. It is in the Word of God. If your faith is based on feeling, or it comes out of your head you will be defeated. Your impossible situation will remain impossible. You can confess until you are blue in the face, and that impossible mountain of financial despair will still be staring you in the face. Because it is coming from your natural faith and not from your spiritual faith.

We talked about natural faith before, but I want to prove that you do have natural faith. Did you check that chair before you sat down in it and began to read this book? Did you check to make sure that it wouldn't fall down before you sat in it? Did you make sure that it is made of good quality material? No! You had faith that that chair would hold you up, and you just plopped down, didn't you?

That is natural faith. If you go out and get into your car to go somewhere, you don't open the hood to see if the motor is still there, and if all the spark plugs are there, and the wires are in place. You don't get something and stick it down in the gasoline tank to see if you have gas. NO! You just jump into the car, put the key in the ignition and turn on the starter, step on the accelerator, and drive off. Your natural human faith causes you to believe that your car is going to take you wherever you wish to go, and it does. On the other hand, if you take that same natural, or human faith, and apply it to impossible spiritual situations, it won't work. Natural human faith isn't supposed to work in the spiritual realm because it is of the physical, natural body realm, and that is where it does work.

You need to get your two faiths figured out.

The kind of faith that works in the spirit realm is the God kind of faith. It makes impossible situations become possible because it is of the spirit, and that is where it is supposed to work. When you get your two faiths figured out, then you can go on to accomplish what you need to accomplish. Too many people have them all mixed together. One time they are in the spirit, and the next time they are in the physical or mental realm. They will make a statement in the natural, and nothing ever happens because they are wavering back and forth. They are vacillating from natural faith to possibility faith.

Until they become established in the Word and make continual statements with this possibility faith, then and only then, will they get results. Then and only then, will they walk and live the victorious life, with no defeats.

If you mix natural faith with spiritual faith, you will have peaks of joy, happiness, and victory, and you will bottom out in the valley of despair. Up and down, up and down; you will peak out again, and then you'll bottom out.

You don't have to live like that. There is a place that you can reach by using the possibility faith that God has given you, and you can live on an even keel. Come what may: whatever happens: let the wind blow: let circumstances come: let the devil roar; you can walk right over the top of every situation that puts itself in your way. Not because you are superhuman, but because the Word of God says so! "All things are possible to him that believeth." Man's impossibilities become God's possibilities through this kind of faith. That is the God kind of faith, or the possibility faith.

A contrast of one who had weak faith and one who used possibility faith, regardless of circumstances.

Here is an example of weak faith. It is found in the Word of God. "The other disciples therefore said unto him, We have seen the Lord. But he (Thomas) said unto them, Except I shall see in his hands the print of the nails, and put my finger into the print of the nails, and thrust my hand into his side, I will not believe. And after eight days again his disciples were within, and Thomas with them: then came Jesus, the doors being shut, and stood in the midst, and said, Peace be unto you. Then saith he to Thomas, Reach hither thy finger, and behold my hands (or put your finger into the nail prints); and reach hither thy hand, and thrust it into my side: and be not faithless, but believing. And Thomas answered and said unto him, My Lord and my God. Jesus saith unto him, Thomas, because thou hast seen me, thou hast believed: blessed are they who have not seen, and yet have believed" (John 20:25–29).

We read in Romans 4:17–21, about a man who had strong faith. "(As it is written, I have made thee a father of many nations,) before him whom he believed, even God, who quickeneth the dead, and calleth those things which be not as though they were. Who against hope believed in hope, that he might become the father of many nations, according to that which was spoken, So shall thy seed be. And being not weak in faith, he considered not his own body now dead, when he was about a hundred years old, neither yet the deadness of Sarah's womb: He staggered not at the promise of God through unbelief; but was strong in faith, giving glory to God; And being fully persuaded that, what he had promised, he was able also to perform." Abraham's strong (heart) faith kept him from looking at the circumstances around him (his and Sarah's age) and getting into unbelief. He knew that God was able and going to perform His Word (He would do what He said that He would do).

Read verse 21 again, "And being fully persuaded that, what He (God) had promised, He was able also to perform." If you are *fully persuaded* that what Jesus has said in the Word of God is true, and what the apostles have written to us in the Word of God concerning believing God is true, you won't be staggering around saying, "Oh, I wonder what's going to happen next?" You will know what is going to happen next, because the Word of God has promised us that if we can only believe, all things are possible.

Jesus said, "Thomas, you believe because you see me, but blessed are those who believe that have not seen me" (Author's paraphrase). Can you see the difference between Thomas' faith and Abraham's faith? Thomas had to see it first, but Abraham exercised his heart faith, and believed what God spoke to him. Abraham didn't even have any children, yet his name was changed from Abram to Abraham, which means *the father of many nations*. Hebrews 11:1 says, "Now faith is. . . . " If faith is not now, it is not faith. **Now faith is.** We read in Romans 4:17 that Abraham believed God. He did not believe according to what he could feel, but he believed according to what was spoken. He had possibility (heart) faith. Possibility faith doesn't look at the impossible situation: it looks at the possible. It calls those things which be not as though they were.

Some people will say, "Well, common sense will tell you . . . Just look at the circumstances; they say thus and so." You have never read anywhere in the Bible that we are told to walk by common sense. It does say that we walk by faith. Possibility faith will get the job done. If Abraham had looked at common sense, he would never have become the father of many nations.

Common sense will tell you that a hundred year old man and a ninety year old woman *ain't ever going to be called "Mama and Papa," if they don't have children already.* But Abraham didn't look at common sense. He said, "I believe as it has been spoken." God had called those things that were not as though they were when He told Abraham that He would make him a father of many nations. He called things that didn't even look possible as though they were. Abraham saw this with his possibility faith, and he took right off behind God, and said, "Well, I believe according to as it is spoken. I am going to be the father of many nations." We are his spiritual descendants. You can read about that in the third chapter of Galatians.

Being moved by what you see, and what you feel will rob you of your efficiency and proficiency. Use your heart faith—possibility faith and speak the Word, then man's impossibilities will become God's possibilities, because the more you exercise your faith, the more it will grow.

When I learned to use my own possibility faith to overcome an impossible situation.

I was born into a family who knew how to believe God. We have believed God all of our lives. We knew what it was to use this *possibility faith* when we were kids. We knew what it was to sit down with Mom and Dad, and to watch a man that knows how to believe God. We would owe thousands of dollars worth of bills, and Dad would go to bed and sleep like a baby, and never be concerned about it. Dad would say, "All right family, we are believing God for so much." We would pray, and we would believe God for that particular situation only one time during our family altar. That was it!

Afterwards, if anybody said anything about it, we would say, "Thank God, the need is met." In fact, we very seldom touched it again, in our prayer life, or thought life. Because as far as we were concerned, it was just like God did it. They spoke and it was so.

Then it happened.

I had never been sick a day in my life. Up until this time, if anything happened to either my sister or me, we called Daddy and he prayed for us. The sad thing was, about all of our family did the same thing. All of his brothers, sisters, cousins, uncles, aunts—everybody. When they got into trouble they would call Kenneth. Kenneth would pray, and they would get healed. After I got older, if they couldn't get hold of Kenneth, they would call on me, and I would have to go pray for them.

We were living in Port Arthur, Texas at the time. I was fifteen years of age and in the ninth grade in Woodrow Wilson Junior High School. Port Arthur is right on the coast, and it is below sea level. I have seen the humidity so high there, that when you lay down on the sheets at night it was as if someone had poured water on the bed. All of a sudden one night my left ear began to hurt so bad that I could hardly stand it. It felt as though somebody had gone to work in there with a buzz saw, a chain saw, or a butcher knife. My father was in California (He was away from home for six to seven weeks at a time: sometimes nine weeks). I got on the phone the next morning and called him. "Daddy," I said, "I've got an earache. Pray for me. There is something bad the matter with my ear. It's more than an earache. There is something bad wrong with it."

For the first time in my life, Dad prayed for me, and nothing happened. I went to my pastor and he prayed for me: nothing happened. Then I found out that Daddy was coming home. "Oh, praise God!" I said, "Daddy's coming home." I got up that morning after having a sleepless night.

Daddy came home and laid hands on me and prayed.

Somebody said, "Who-o-o, you got it!" No I didn't. In fact, I wished that he hadn't prayed for me. I felt worse than I did before he prayed. Dad went to the East coast somewhere, preaching. My ear was *not any better!* And for the first time in my life, I went to the doctor (for something other than a physical examination, required by the school if anyone wished to participate in sports).

The doctor said, "Son, you have an ear fungus. It comes from the South Sea Islands, and because you have irritated it by rubbing it, you have caused sores to get down in there like boils. Now, we can *sort of* stop it, and heal the sores up, but this fungus that grows in there will never heal up. It is incurable. It grows in wet, damp climates, and if it is left alone, it will eventually eat up all of your hearing." He said, "There are some extreme cases where this fungus has eaten out of the ear canal, and right on through the skull when it wasn't taken care of." He told me again, "We can't cure it, but we can control it, but as long as you live down here you will have to have your ear cleaned out every week." The doctor took a little instrument and stuck it down in my ear. When he turned it, some tiny blades came out, and he worked it around and pulled out all that mess that was in my ear. Then he took a long piece of cotton, dipped in a chartreuse colored oily substance, and stuffed it down in my ear. He gave me a small bottle of the stuff and said,

"Ok, keep that cotton soaked up with that." He went on to say, "Don't ever swim again. Don't ever get your head under water again. Even be careful washing around your ear, to be sure that very little moisture gets in that ear." He said, "If you move out in the desert, you might get by with having your ear cleaned out once every month or six weeks. But for the rest of your life, you are going to have to have it cleaned out."

I took the medicine and went home. That was the first time that we ever had medicine in our house. There is nothing wrong with medicine, if you need it. Praise God, take it until you can get enough faith in you to where you don't have to take it. I am not against medicine, and I am not against doctors. If you are sick and can't get your healing because your faith is not developed enough, I will take you to the hospital myself, and I will keep you alive until I get enough faith in you to where you can believe God.

Doctors are fighting the devil the same as I; only they are using natural means, and I am using divine means. We are fighting the same diseases. A lot of good doctors have kept a lot of people alive until they got enough of the Word in them to believe for their healing. Don't ever let it be said that any of the Hagins are against doctors. In fact, there wouldn't be any of this Hagin line if the doctors had not taken care of one of them until he got enough faith to walk off that bed. They told him that he was going to die, but they did all they could for him while he was in that condition. They did all that they could do, and then he walked off of there healed because God's Word says so.

It was somewhere around Christmas time, when the great faith prophet came home. I asked him if he would take me to the doctor to get my ear cleaned out. I had been going about twice a week, and because the doctor could not help me, he was not charging me anything. I would go to his office after he had taken his last patient, just before he went to lunch. It did not take very long. I would just jump out of the car and run right up to the doctor's office, and by the time that Dad drove around the block, I was ready to jump in, and away we would go. I was lounging against the side of the door, my eyes were barely level with the glass in the door, and Dad said, "Son, do you want to be healed?"

Now wasn't that crazy? I had asked him to pray for me twice; the pastor had prayed for me, and here he was taking me to the doctor, and he asked me if I wanted to get healed!

"Sure," I replied.

He said, "I can tell you how."

There we were driving down the street toward home, and I am waiting, waiting, waiting, and finally, I said, "How?"

He said, "I thought you would never ask, and I didn't want to waste my breath. If you didn't want to know, I wasn't going to tell you." Man—that's the way he is too! He said, "I was praying about this situation, and the Lord showed me that you know as much about faith as just about anybody. You've been around this thing all of your life. You've been on the platform since you were two years old. You have heard me preach, and you have seen the power of God. You know it. The Lord even says that you have been preaching some of my sermons."

I said, "Oh, yeah. Down there the other day at the Youth Meeting we were supposed to have a big service, and the speaker didn't show up. They were all nervous, wondering what they were going to do, and I told them, 'You get up and you have the singing and the special music, and if the speaker hasn't showed, you just turn it to me. I'll handle this job. Don't you worry about it.'"

I got up there and I preached one of Dad's sermons. He calls it, "How to Write Your Own Ticket With God." If you have ever listened to any of his tapes or read it in his material, you know that there are four simple rules to go by: *Say it. Do it. Believe it. And receive it.*

I told him, "Sure, I've been preaching."

He said, "The Lord told me you had." He went on, "Now, if you want to get healed you are going to have to exercise your faith, and receive with your faith from your heart."

The time had come for me to exercise my own faith.

I was facing an impossible situation, and everybody had prayed for me, and I didn't get anything. The time had come that I was going to have to change my impossible situation into a possible situation by using my own possibility faith. You know, when you first get over into this thing, every time you pray and every time that somebody prays for you, it will happen. But there comes a time when God expects you to grow up, and use your own possibility faith to get what you want from Him. I had been telling those young people how to receive whatever they wanted from God, simply by using those four principles, yet I was expecting somebody else to carry me. It hit me like a rock.

There are many people who are in the faith message today. They have heard faith, after faith, after faith, preacher and teacher, and yet they are not receiving from God.

If you are not receiving from God, it is because you are not putting your faith that you know, and the faith that you have in your heart, into action. You are not actually believing for yourself. You are wanting somebody else to believe for you. It is not because it's not God's will to heal you.

I can't understand some people. They will say, "Well, maybe it's not the will of God for me to get healed." Yet, they go to every doctor in the country to try to get healed. If it is not the will of God for them to be healed, then I ask you, why are they trying to get healed? I have been taught that we are supposed to be in the will of God.

I knew what to do. I knew that I had heart faith. I had heard it preached all of my life, but I just had never exercised my own faith. You understand—I had faith, but I never exercised it. When we got home, Daddy said, "Do you want to pray?"

"Sure," I said, and we knelt down in the front room, and I waited, and waited, and waited. Daddy didn't say a word. Finally, I asked, "Are you going to pray?"

He said, "No. It isn't me that needs anything. I'm just here to *scotch* for you."

He was using a colloquial expression that you perhaps have used when you have jacked up a car and said, "Hey, get a piece of brick, or wood, and *block* the wheels so it won't roll."

He meant that when I said, "Amen," he was going to throw his faith up behind mine so it wouldn't move. I prayed a simple prayer based on Mark 11:23: saying it with my mouth because I believed it in my heart. I was exercising the possibility faith, and I immediately got up from there, went directly into the bathroom, took that cotton out of my ear, and flushed it down the commode.

You may say, "Oh! it was healed."

No, it wasn't healed. When that cold, damp air hit my ear, it felt like somebody just drove a knife in there and started twisting it around. I was calling those things which were not as though they were. I took the medicine and threw it away. I changed my clothes and went out to the vacant lot where our neighborhood ball team was playing the boys from the south part of town. We played tackle football without using pads.

I came prancing up as I said, "Ok, I'm here!"

They said, "Why, we thought you couldn't play ball any more, Hagin."

"Well, I'm here. I'm well," I said.

"You sure don't look like it."

"I'm well, thank you. Do you want me to play, or don't you?"

"Oh yeah. Get in your right halfback spot."

I said, "Fine, thank you. Call the play and let's get on with it." They had already had the kickoff. The quarterback said, "Look, they've got a weak defensive end, and the linebacker is slow as molasses. Our end from the other side can go downfield and cut down the safety man, and you are going to have clear sailing down the sideline."

I said, "Fine. Let's get on with it." We came bopping out there. He pitched the ball over to me, and that defensive end came crashing in. We just went around him and let him go. The linebacker was trying to move over, and about that time one of the guys in front of me just pushed him out of the way, and I saw our man coming across from the other side. He took out the safety man, and it was just clear sailing, and I was hooking 'em down the sideline. Out of the corner of my eye, I saw somebody coming at an angle, and I reached back and called for a little extra reserve, and I didn't have it. I didn't have any reserve because I hadn't been working out.

That is what happens to you with your faith when you need a little extra, and you reach back for it, and it isn't there because you haven't been exercising it. You haven't been keeping your faith up.

Well, that's what happened to me. I reached back for a little bit more speed, and I hadn't been exercising for a couple of months, so he caught me. He came up and grabbed me in one of those headlocks. Of course he came from the side and he got my left ear right on his hip. He started rolling it around, and I was still trying to run. Finally, I went to the ground just to get him to turn loose of my head. He didn't put me down! I went down. It was hurting. But I said, "I'm healed. Thank God, I am well. I'm healed."

Now, I want you to realize that I was having to exercise my possibility faith. I hadn't been exercising it. I knew how to make it work but I hadn't been doing it.

When you get yourself in that kind of situation, the devil is going to find out whether you really believe what you say you believe or not. He is not going to *tuck tail and run*. He will stand there and bow his neck, and growl and howl. He will give you all kind of threats, because he is going to find out if you really believe what God's Word says—that when it's impossible with man, it is possible with God, and all things are possible to him who believes.

I kept saying the Word.

For two weeks, every time that I turned around, I was saying, "I am healed by the power of God." I was exercising this possibility faith of my heart, and not of my head. If I had been exercising with my head, I would have done what my head wanted to do. I would have gone back to the doctor, and got me some more medicine, because at least, it kept the pain from hurting so much. At least, when the wind would hit into that thing, it wouldn't hurt. But I kept confessing. I went back to school after the Christmas vacation, and it was the boys' turn to use the olympic size swimming pool in Physical Education class. Now was the opportunity to put my **possibility faith** to its final test. I was told by the physician never to put my head under water again. I got down in the pool, and I put my nose on one of those black lines on the bottom of the pool, and I swam to the deep end of the pool. Every time that I took a stroke, common sense would say, "You ought not to be doing this, boy."

My heart on the inside was saying, "Thank God, I'm well. I am healed! I have no pain. I have no ear trouble so therefore I can swim!"

My head was hollering at me, "Why, you stupid thing. Don't you know how bad your ear hurts? The first time that you got water in it—don't you know? Look here, you are down underneath this water, and it is just flowing in that ear. You are stupid, boy!"

My heart on the inside kept saying, "Thank God. The Word of God says I am healed. I am whole by the stripes of Jesus Christ. The Word says, 'All things are possible to him that believeth.' The Word says, 'When it is impossible with man, it is possible with God.' The Word says, 'If I'll have this kind of possibility faith that will move mountains, I can be healed of this thing.'"

I kept saying, "The Word says I am healed," all the way to the other end. "I'll put my nose right against the wall on the other end." I backed off and went out as far as I could go, and I shot for the top of the pool. When I hit the top of the water, something popped inside my head, and I said, "Thank God, I am healed."

About that time, all the rest of the kids had gotten in the pool. "What did you say?" they asked.

"I said, Thank God, I am healed," I answered them. They looked at me as if I were crazy. I didn't care. I had just won my victory, and I want to tell you this. From that day to this, the enemy has never been able to put sickness and disease on me. And he never will, because I have learned how to turn impossible situations into possible situations by believing the Word of God.

The Word says, "All things are possible to him that believeth."

The Word says, "When it's impossible with man, it is possible with God."

The Word says, "Nothing shall be impossible to you, and you can have what God says, with this possibility faith." You don't get it sometime. That puts it in the future. The Word says, "Now faith is." Faith is now. Possibility faith is now.

A fellow once said to my Dad, "Well, I'm not going to believe something that I can't see or feel."

Dad asked him, "Have you got any brains? Have you ever seen them? Have you ever felt them?"

"Aw," he said, "that's a different thing."

"No it's not," Dad said. "Just as sure as you have some brains in that head of yours, the Word of God works."

If you look in the 11th chapter of Hebrews, you will find Abraham's picture in the gallery of the heroes of faith, but you won't find Thomas' picture there. I'm not discrediting Thomas, because (according to church history) he went on to do some great work for God. But I am showing you that in these two particular cases, Thomas' faith came from his head. He was operating in the impossibility faith. He said, "I won't believe until I can touch, feel, and see." And Abraham operated in his possibility faith. He said, "I call those things which be not as though they were, because God did, and I believe according to as it was spoken. I am the father of many nations."

Somebody said, "Where are your kids, Abraham?"

Old Abraham would answer, "I believe according to as it is spoken."

"But, where are your kids, Abraham?"

"I believe according to as it was spoken, it shall be. I am fully persuaded that He that has promised will make it come to pass."

"Where are your kids, Abraham?"

"Oh, they are all over now—see!"

When you face the problems of life, and the circumstances scream around you, where is your answer?

You can scream right back with the Word of God, "I am not moved by what I see or what I feel. I am moved only by what the Word says, and the Word says, 'I am healed by His stripes.' The Word says, 'All of my needs are met according to His riches in glory.'"

That possibility faith quotes the Word, and walks through life victoriously, singing *Standing on the Promises, I shall prevail, when the howling storms of doubt and fear assail. Standing on the promises, I'll be an overcomer.*

What to do if you have an impossible situation.

If you have an impossible situation in your life that you want changed, think of a Scripture verse from the Word of God that covers your case. Say this: "Father, the Word of God says that when it is impossible with man, it is possible with God. The Word says that all things are possible to him that believeth. The Word says that nothing shall be impossible to me. Now Father, I thank you that this impossible situation has become a possibility. The mountain of impossibility has been moved, and the need is met. Now, according to the Word of God. . . . (quote your Scripture verse to Him, and thank Him for it). Faith thanks now. Faith acts now. Right now is when it is happening! Now is the time to get excited over it. Faith gets excited now. After it happens it is "old hat." Praise God! Faith is now.

I know of a man who on a Monday night prayed for his wife to get saved. A week went by, and another week, and on the last night of the meeting (Sunday), his wife went to the altar to get saved. All the rest of the church was jumping up and down, shouting and praising God, and the husband just sat there and looked around. "What's the matter with you?" someone said. "That's your wife down there. She's getting saved!"

He said, "Well, didn't you see me on that first Monday night of this meeting? I was jumping and hollering, and having a good time! That's the time she got saved in my book—when I put my faith on it."

It happens in the spiritual realm right when you call it into existence, and it manifests itself in the natural realm, later. That experience is already over, and you are ready for another, praise God!

Continue to say, "Thank you God, that impossible situation is possible through the Word." Keep quoting the Word. Keep quoting the Word. Keep quoting the Word, and let your possibility faith grow to a higher level.

CHAPTER 4

Possibility Faith: When Will It Work for Others?

Christians need to take their places in the Word of God, then they will find that there is no need for them to dwell in the house of the impossible. There has been made a way of escape, and that is through possibility faith from the Word of God.

Possibility faith will always work for you, but it will not always work for others. Sometimes, it will: sometimes, it won't. This causes you to ask, "Well, it works for me, why can't I always make my faith work for others?"

Well, that is the subject that we are going to pursue in this last chapter. If you will do a study of this, you will find that you can receive by faith in the Word of God, healing, prosperity, and all of your needs, plus "Whatsoever things you desire." I wish to point out that your desire may not be the same as Grandpa's. You may desire that Grandpa have something, but Grandpa may not want it. The Bible doesn't say, "Whatsoever things Sister, or Daddy desires." It says, "Whatsoever *you* desire. . . . " It is a personal thing. It doesn't matter how strong your faith is, you cannot push your desires off onto other members of your family, or friends, if they don't want them. You can't push salvation off on people against their will. You can pray and intercede, or plead their case for them, but until they decide that they want salvation, and they take the Word of God like it tells us to do in Romans 10:9,10 they will not be saved.

Neither can God make anybody get saved above their own will. If He could do that, there would be no use in us hanging around down here any longer. He could make everybody in the world get saved and take us on to heaven. The Word of God says that each of us have been made free moral agents. We are free spirits, who can choose whether or not we will serve God. We also have the choice of whether or not we will walk in the faith life.

You can be saved, filled with the Holy Spirit, and go on to heaven, and never walk in the faith life. Some people believe that if you don't walk—strong in faith, you won't make it to heaven. Of course that is not true. As long as you have enough faith to look up, and in the face of God, quote Romans 10:9,10 you can be saved, whether or not you ever believe God for one copper penny, or anything else in this life. You can get to heaven simply by believing for salvation, because salvation is the criterion that gets you to heaven.

Getting into the family of God is similar to getting into your own natural family. When you were born into your family, and after you grew some, did you keep asking for something that you wanted from the refrigerator when you could get it for yourself? If you want milk or cereal, you should (after you grow tall enough to reach the door handles!) get it for yourself. If you want a peanut butter and jelly sandwich, you should go get the bread, jelly, and peanut butter and fix it for yourself. You see, everything belongs to you because you are part of the family, but whether or not you take advantage of your privilege is up to you. It is the same when you are born into the family of God. Everything here belongs to you, but whether or not you take advantage of your privileges (through faith) is up to you.

Locate the person that you wish to help—faith-wise.

Suppose you are trying to help a certain man in his faith walk. Healing belongs to him already if he is a Christian. All of the things of God belong to him, just as they belong to you. But the first thing that you must do is to make certain that he has had enough faith to be saved. After you are sure that he is saved, you need to locate him *faith-wise*. Is his faith up to the level to where he can agree with you? If you are believing for his healing and he is believing that he is going to die, the two of you are not in agreement, and you will have to get him turned around.

You don't do this by going in there and hounding him like this: "Boy, have faith in God. God will heal you, have faith in God." That is what you want to get over to him, but that is not the most diplomatic approach to use to get him into the area of receiving.

If he is a *bona fide baby Christian,* more than likely your possibility faith will work for him. If he is a *programmed older Christian,* he may have some traditional barriers to hurdle before you can get in agreement.

If you pray for somebody in the area of healing, and you go over and say, "Well, is it done?"

If he replies, "Well, I sure hope so." He is not healed because he is hoping and you are believing, and that won't work. You need to get him to listen to some good faith messages, or read a good faith book. He needs something to build his faith. Now don't go out there and get any of those testimonies that they print up that say, "The Lord caused all of this stuff to happen to me." That is a bunch of baloney. Get some good testimonies.

Many people won't listen to somebody preach. Some won't read a book, but if you will get some good testimonies of somebody who has been delivered and been set free; they will usually read these, because they are really interesting. People like to read about others who have made a success, or have overcome obstacles. You can get people to read these when they won't read anything else.

After you get them reading those testimonies you can slip in a little faith book, and say, "I have something else here that is really great. I would like you to read it." Don't throw a big hunk of faith food at them, right off the bat. Remember, they aren' used to that.

If you can just get his faith built up to where he, at least, can be in agreement with you, you can use your faith to help him. You don't have to build that individual up to your level of faith to accomplish this. If you can just get him to the level that he will say, "I believe that it is so, and I will agree with you."

The babies in the church need care.

The Bible teaches similarity between physical growth and spiritual growth. A few years back, my dad was holding a revival for a certain minister, and they had been having tremendous results in the altar services. One particular night many young couples were saved. Only a few of them had ever been in church before. Someone asked the pastor if anybody got their names and addresses. And to make a long story short, he said, "Oh, I just thought if they got anything they would be back."

That is the equivalent of a family going to the hospital and they have a baby. Then everybody goes home, and somebody comes over to see the new baby, and asks, "Well, where is the baby?"

The parents answer, "Oh, if it's alive it will be home after while."

That sounds peculiar, but that is exactly what we do to babies who are born into the family of God. We just leave them to shift for themselves. "Bless God, if they got anything they will be back." And if they do come back, we stick them in a class where there is a bunch of spiritually mature people, and the teacher gets up there and puts out spiritual food that literally chokes them to death. They can't swallow it, and they begin to dry up and die of malnutrition.

It is silly to think that new baby Christians can just take care of themselves.

Some will say, "That isn't my job. Let the pastor do it." Listen, the pastor is too busy taking care of the old spiritual babies to take care of the new ones.

This is where we, as the older brothers and sisters in Christ, in particular fellowship, should begin to minister.

There is a teaching concerning "body ministry," and I am not talking or teaching that. However, there is a place for the body ministry. It is not to the extremes that some have carried it.

Here is where the correct body ministry comes in: *The elder brothers and sisters in the Lord, minister in the fellowship, underneath the shepherds.* I am talking about the shepherds that it talks about in the Word of God. The undershepherds under Jesus Christ, the chief Shepherd.

Somebody said, "Well I don't see any covering."

Bless God, look over your heads, and you will see the Word. That is our covering. The covering of the blood of the Lord Jesus Christ, and the Word of God is our cover!

And that is all the cover we need. We don't have to have an umbrella.

It is time that we, as the true believers begin to take our stand, and stand for the things that are right. We don't have to get into strife over it: we can love the brothers and still not be in tune with what they are teaching.

Paul tells us in Romans 16:17, "Now I beseech you, brethren, mark them which cause divisions and offences contrary to the doctrine which ye have learned; and avoid them." Do what Paul is telling you here, but don't hold any strife against anybody.

Programmed and unprogrammed spiritual babies.

You have seen a new babe in Christ come into the fold, and the pastor may begin to use pastoral love to help this individual over some rough places. He may even take him out to dinner, and have a little fellowship with him. And one of the other saints in the fellowship may say, "Well, I just can't understand it. Brother Ed went out with So-and-so, and he never has been out to dinner with us."

Many times when you see pastors, and others fellow-shipping with certain ones, they aren't doing it just to be fellowshipping. They are ministering the way that they are supposed to be doing, to get that individual grown up in the Lord, and through his babyhood stage. They do this so he can learn and get involved, and either catch up, or surpass some of the church members who have been sitting around griping. Remember, if you are griping you are not learning. You have stopped moving forward, and started looking at everything around about you. When you are moving forward, you have your eyes out there on the goal in front of you. You don't have time to notice the things that are going on around you, because you are concerned with the ministry in front of you. You need to keep confessing the Word and keep walking, because it is when you stop, and start looking around you, that you get into all these other areas and avenues.

As long as people are spiritual babies you can carry them. It is comparatively easy to get people healed when you go into a place where people have not been taught, and they do not have a bunch of programmed and preconceived ideas on healing. It is easy to go on a missionary crusade, and preach to thousands of people: to preach Jesus Christ the healer to them, and just give them the simple basics of faith. You don't even have to put your hands on them and pray with them. They will start jumping up all over the place because they simply believe what you have told them.

If you give me a choice of a crowd of 25 people on a foreign field, or a crowd of 25,000 Americans who have been programmed, I'll take the former every time. Because I will get more results out of the 25 than I will out of the 25,000 that have been programmed with all kinds of nonsense.

If you find an unprogrammed individual, it is easy to talk to that one about faith, and he will start working his faith immediately. A young Rhema student (Rhema Bible

Training College—Broken Arrow, Oklahoma) came into my office one day, and said, "I can't understand why so many are having trouble believing God for money, and everything else."

I said, "Well, what are you talking about?"

He said, "Well, it's like this. I have never been to church in my life, and I didn't know anything about the Word of God, but it is easy for me to believe. I never ask for anything that I don't get."

Here is the important thing: He had no preconceived ideas about faith, or believing God, or how anything was supposed to be. So—when somebody told him about believing God, he simply started doing it, and it worked.

"Why!" he said, "I am never without!" He couldn't understand why some who had been around the faith message for a while were having trouble receiving.

I explained to him, that even though they had been around it for a while, they were so programmed that they don't even know how to use their own faith. And when they did receive a few things in the beginning, they had received them on somebody else's faith. Now, since they are hearing the Word, they have to stand on their own two feet, and they don't know what they are doing. So many who have gotten into the faith message are floundering because they haven't been taught properly about receiving, and how to make their faith work for them. When they first got into the faith message everything started working, then all of a sudden it shut down on them, and they couldn't figure out what was going on. They are still getting people to pray with them, but the time has come when God expects them to use their own possibility faith, and the pastor and friends can no longer carry them.

Your faith will work for others for a time.

Here is an example of someone else's faith working for members of my family, until the time came when they needed to use their own faith, and agree with the one doing the praying. My cousin came to live with us when she was fifteen years old, and she lived with us until she married. She married a young Baptist boy, when she was out of fellowship with God. I am not saying anything against the Baptists, but there are many people in every church that say they are *this*, when they really aren't anything. My cousin said that she was *Pentecostal*, but she wasn't going to church anywhere.

They moved to Houston, and she had gotten back in fellowship with God. Early one morning the phone rang. And I remember Dad saying, "Well, who is this?" Finally, I heard him say, "Quiet down, what's the matter?" It was Dad's only sister.

By that time, everybody in the house was awake. Sis, Mom, and I ran over to Dad and asked, "What is it? What's gone wrong?"

"Well," Daddy said, "Your cousin's baby is born, and they said that he was born dead at first, and then they said that he wasn't dead, but he didn't have oxygen, and he is so deformed that he doesn't even look like a human in the face. . . . It will be better if nobody ever sees him, and they want me to pray." See—they know who to call on when they need something!

Dad knew how to put his *possibility faith* to work on the *impossible situation,* and he said, "Tell them that the baby will live and not die; it will be all right."

My aunt said, "Oh, you think so, Kenneth?"

"No, I don't think it—I know it. Now repeat after me. . . . " Daddy had her repeat it again, then he said, "As soon as you hang up this phone, you tell them what I said."

The next day, when everybody finally arrived at the hospital, my cousin's husband met them shouting, "I am a Pentecostal-Baptist!" You see it wasn't ten minutes after my aunt hung up that phone, when the nurse came out and said, "You can see the baby now. We don't know what happened, but all of a sudden his head blew out like you would blow up a balloon, and the baby is all right." That was a miracle. They had just seen the power of God at work. But a small bone was missing, and he was going to have to undergo an extensive operation (a bone transplant).

He is a healthy grown boy now, but I want to show you something. Somebody else's faith (Dad's) had worked for them and saved that child's life.

I have seen uncles, aunts, great uncles—all of them in our family, call on Dad for prayer, when we would be at all places in the United States.

One time Dad's mother (my grandmother) called and said that Dad's first cousin was in the hospital, "And the doctor says that she isn't going to live."

Dad knew they didn't know anything about faith. In fact, at that time, they didn't even claim to be Christians.

Dad said, "Well, you just tell them, Momma, that she will live and not die." Her whole body was one mass of infection, and it was just a matter of time. As soon as the infection reached her heart she would die. The infection had already deadened her legs.

Grandma said, "Oh, you have heard from heaven!" She knew that Daddy had special manifestations from on high.

"Sure have!" he said.

"Oh, praise the Lord!" she exclaimed.

"Mark 11:23 says. . . . "

"Oh," she said as she sounded disappointed.

Everybody wants some spiritual manifestation—some audible voice, or something that will give them a sign. They have all the sign that they will ever need. It is in the Word: "Say it with your mouth, believe it in your heart, and watch it happen."

Believers need to grow up, spiritually.

I watched members of our family as they were healed, time and time again: instant things. And then, I saw the day come when they called for help and nothing happened.

We prayed, we said it, and nothing happened. This is when Brother Hagin, my dad, began to study on this, and I picked it up from listening to him. Dad gets into this in his book, *Growing Up Spiritually.*[2] He began to explain it this way. We will take care of a physical baby for a while. But we expect that child to grow up and start feeding and taking care of itself. God will work for people for a while, but the day will come when He expects Christians to quit having someone else spoon-feed them, and start believing for themselves. They need to grow up to the faith level of agreeing with someone else.

Your faith will work for them if their desires are the same as yours, when they are baby Christians, but they are soon going to have to believe God for themselves.

It is sad to say, but many people never learn the facts of using their own faith until they have faced a tragic situation, and they call on God and nothing happens. Then, they begin to search and pray, and seek God. They begin to look into the Word of God, and they find out that it was their own fault.

Don't blame God.

People keep blaming God for the bad things that happen to them. It's not His fault. Once, while I was teaching in a certain city, a tragedy struck. Some children had been missing for over four hours, and they were hit by a train. It was not the train company's fault. It was their train, and it was on their track, and the engineer was doing his job. And neither was it God's fault. The fault lay in the fact that the parents didn't even know where the kids were. It took them four hours of knocking on doors in the neighborhood, before they found them. The fault went back to the parents. The kids shouldn't have been playing on the railroad track.

Now, the parents probably told them not to play there, but since they were minors, it was up to the parents to keep them away.

God has already told us in His Word: "Nothing is impossible to him that believeth," and "When it is impossible with men, it is possible with God." But people won't accept what He is telling them to do. And they go their own way instead of God's way, and they get into trouble. Then, they will either blame God, or the devil, when neither of them had anything to do with it.

They will say, "Oh, the devil did it."

Well, if the devil did it, it was because you allowed him to do it.

It is up to you.

Possibility faith will work for you if you will work it, but it is up to you to make it work. It would be silly for me to sit down and hold my pencil in my hand and say, "I wonder how much 2 X 6 is?" and I just sit there as I say, "I learned the multiplication tables but they just won't work for me. Now, I wonder how much 2 X 6 is?" Of course, you know how to make the multiplication tables work for yourself, and you know that 2 X 6 = 12. That is the way it is with possibility faith. It doesn't work by itself. You have to make it work for you. You already have the formula.

You learned a formula in the principles of mathematics for finding the circumference of a circle. You learned a formula for finding the radius of a circle. You learned a formula for finding the diameter of a circle. And you learned a formula for finding the volume of a cylinder. If you took mathematics in school, you learned the formula for each of those things, but until you take some paper and a pencil and go to work, those formulas will not work for you.

If you have a little pocket calculator, you can get it to work for you, but you have to—at least, push the buttons. I am sure that some day, modern technology will come up with a calculator that you will only have to speak to and it will work, but you still will have to speak to it. That is the way it is with possibility faith. It is up to you to make it work for yourself.

Possibility faith will always work for you, and sometimes it will work for others when they fall into certain categories, but it will never work for somebody when their desire is not the same as yours. Possibility faith will never work for them if they don't want or agree to be healed, regardless of how badly you want to deliver them.

One of the *gifts of the Spirit* may start operating, and they could be healed that way, but that is another subject entirely, and people need to be taught on that. There is a difference between the operation of the *gifts of the Spirit,* and special anointing where faith has to be exercised. When the *gifts of the spirit,* working of miracles, and other gifts are in operation, things just happen. But when it is a special anointing or where you are wanting something for yourself, you—YOU have to activate the power of God with your faith. Jesus didn't tell the woman with the issue of blood, in Mark 5: "Daughter, my power has made you whole." No! He turned around and said, "Thy faith hath made thee whole." *Your faith: your faith.* That woman took her possibility faith, and turned an impossibility into a possibility.

How did she do that?

When she heard.

When she heard what?

When she heard the Word. The first chapter of John's Gospel, verse 14, says that *the Word was made flesh and dwelt among us.* It is the written Word. When she had heard. "Faith cometh by hearing and hearing and hearing and hearing the Word of God" (Author's paraphrase). You can't put too many of them in this verse of Scripture.

This method works in the natural as well as the spiritual realm. Psychologists will tell a person who has no confidence in himself to take a pencil and a piece of paper, and write his name over, and over, and over again. They will also say, "Stand in front of a mirror and look at yourself, and say your name, to yourself—out loud, over and over, and over again."

Take the Word of God and build your confidence. "Cast not away your confidence. . . . " (Hebrews 10:35). The Word is your confidence. The Word makes possibility faith and therefore all things become possible to you because there never has, and there never will be impossibilities with God. Possibility after possibility exists if you will cause them to come into reality. Possibilities exist as the children of God speak them forth from their mouths.

I have never been around an impossible situation, because where the power of God is there is all sufficient power to take care of any problem that arises.

Take that power and the Word, and speak forth what you desire, and watch it happen in your life.

Quote the Word over those you wish to help.

If you are going to help anybody else to believe, you have to get them *up* in faith, to where they will believe, and it has to be their desire.

What if they don't want salvation?

Then quote the Word over them. It says in Hebrews 11:6, " . . . he that cometh to God must believe that he is. . . . " Find some Word to quote over them so they will start believing in God. Then, when they start believing in God, the Holy Spirit will help. Their will will change. Until they believe in God all of your praying, and all of your confessions won't do any good, because you are putting it down the wrong channel.

I am not telling you that it's impossible for them to find God the way that you are going about it. You are not using the right formula. If I want to find the radius of a circle, I can get it by finding the diameter, but I have to do something else. I will have to divide the diameter in half. You see, I have to do some adjusting. It is the same when you are dealing with that lost person. You may start out using one area of believing, and when you get into it you will realize where that individual is, and you will say, "Hey! this is not the right formula." And you will have to go back and adjust.

Sometimes when we start out using this possibility faith we get into the situation and we may have thought that the person was believing with us, and all of a sudden, we find that they are only hoping. We are believing, and they are only hoping. We have to change and adjust so that we can bring them up to where they can get in agreement with us, before we can get the answer.

Possibilities exist where impossible situations are found.

The impossible brings great victories.

The trial of faith brings great rewards. There has never been a victory where there was not a battle.

Don't think that you are going to get up from reading this book and just start using that possibility faith, and things will start happening for you—right and left, because they are not.

You may say, "Ken, you build us up, and then you take all the air out of us."

Well good! That will keep your feet on the ground when you finish the book, and then you can get something accomplished!

Victory Boulevard or Defeat Street—it's up to you.

I want you to know that you can take this possibility faith and make things work for you. And I also want you to know that before you ever stop reading, the devil is not going to give up that easily. He is going to find out whether you really believe that all things are possible to him that believeth. He is going to make you work the formula before he will *tuck tail and run*.

This has been the downfall of many good people who have turned their backs on the faith message: They have walked out and started using some principles that they have heard taught, and they had a little bit of opposition. Everything wasn't just rosy and beautiful, and they said, "Well, this stuff isn't worth it." They were snared by the words of their mouths. You talk about cowed, beaten individuals, that is what you find.

If you can get them back to the place where they will confess the Word—properly—with their mouths; the way they are supposed to, and fight through to the victory, you will find that they will never be defeated again, as long as they live.

Once you have tasted the thrill of victory, you are never satisfied with the agony of defeat. In this life, in spiritual or natural things—whatever, once you have tasted the thrill of being on top, you will never go back to the bottom.

Perhaps, in your job, you have worked your way up through the ranks. Promotion after promotion, and you are on the top now. You are going to make sure that you will never have to be back down there on the bottom again.

When I was in the army I became a squad leader, and when I went overseas, I was promoted to the assistant in charge of our whole outfit (working in the communication center). I guarantee you, I made sure that I didn't get back down where I had to pull KP (kitchen police), and clean latrines. I made sure that I stayed up on top, because I liked the privileges that went with the rank.

I like the privileges that go with the rank of the soldier of the Lord Jesus Christ. I have learned to use the possibility faith, and I am going to fight the battle with the Word of God, and stay on top. I am going to stay the victor. I am going to be an overcomer in Christ Jesus. I have been down there on Defeat Street, and I'm not going back there. I am going to continue to live on Victory Boulevard.

Somebody said, "Yeah, but common sense will tell you that you have to come down sometime."

I'm not moved by common sense! The Word of God says that I live by faith, and not common sense.

"Yeah, but circumstances say so and so."

I'm not moved by circumstances. I'm not moved by what I feel. I'm not moved by what I see. I'm not moved by anything except what I believe. And I believe what the Word says.

The Word says, "Greater is He that is in me than he that is in the world."

The Word says, "By His stripes I am healed."

The Word says, "According to His riches in glory by Christ Jesus, all of my needs are supplied." And that means *an abundant supply,* and not just a *get-by.*

The Word says. That is how you make possibility faith work. It is how you create possibilities out of impossibilities.

Remember this. Write it down.

If you do not remember anything else that you have read, remember this: **The Word of God will make possibilities out of impossibilities.**

As an associate pastor in youth work, back in the 60's, I got the kids to make posters: *"Greater Is He That Is In Me Than He That Is In The World;" "I Am A Victor,"* etc. I had them hang the posters so that the first thing they saw when they walked into the room, and the last thing they saw when they walked out was that poster. If you have to, make a sign with these words on it: *Through the Word of God, impossibilities are possibilities.* Put it where it is the first thing you see in the morning, and the last thing you see at night. Say it over and over to yourself. If you say it no more than those two times—after a while, you will find that suddenly things are different for you.

It will be because you have been confessing that through the Word of God impossibilities are possibilities. You will have then schooled yourself into possibility faith.

MAN'S IMPOSSIBILITIES— GOD'S POSSIBILITIES!

---

[2] Kenneth E. Hagin, Growing Up Spiritually, Kenneth Hagin Ministries; Tulsa, Oklahoma, 1976.